This book is dedicated to my family,

who inspire me to try new ideas and are so willing to eat

those that go wrong in the trialling process!

Photographs Copyright © J. Arrowsmith 2018

www.mindthegapsdiet.weebly.com

Contents

Introduction

For health reasons we have been eating grain-free as a family for a while now. We have been following the GAPS diet.

One of the things I love to do is to take our old favourite grain/sugar full recipes and make them grain-free and refined sugar-free.

I hope, with this small collection, to inspire you to dig out your old recipe books and see what you can adapt.

I don't like having to source 'strange' ingredients, nor can we afford lots of eggs/special flours and nuts etc. so most of my recipes use a lot of courgette.

Yes, courgette. It makes for a very versatile ingredient. You can substitute butternut squash instead, but I find courgette so cheap (especially in season and if you grow your own!) and easy to prepare.

So how do I work with courgette? I use it as a flour substitute and as such it reduces the amount of coconut flour I need in a recipe. This is turn reduces the number of eggs required. Many cake recipes using coconut flour require 6 eggs a time. These bakes need only three. It also reduces the amount of fibre - a consideration for those on a gut healing diet. Courgette also produces a lovely spongey, moist texture. An added bonus is a reduction in carbs too.

A food processor is essential for all of these recipes.

I recommend that you add the ingredients in the order suggested and make the cake all at once - don't leave it sitting in the pan half finished while you do another job as it will dry up. Coconut flour is very absorbent.

Always store your courgette bakes in the fridge in an air-tight container, for up to a week.

If your cake sinks - don't worry, it will still be edible, but maybe next time try smaller eggs.

If it is too dry, make sure you have not left it sitting too long before baking, or consider adding more moisture next time. All ovens bake differently too, so work out your own cooking time using my guide.

The quick way to prepare courgette

1. Peel and slice the courgette.

2. Stack up the slices ...

3. Run the knife downwards through the slices.

4. Turn the stack 90 degrees and slice downwards again.

5. Fill a cup with the quarters.

Ingredients
and Measures

Coconut flour - best organic and sourced from a health food shop where the prices are often cheaper then superstores. I measure with a measuring cup.

Desiccated coconut - best to buy organic and sourced from a health food shop where the prices are cheaper than superstores. Watch out for hidden preservatives. I measure this with a measuring cup.

Dried fruit - Best to buy organic if possible, but we can't always afford organic so ordinary will do just as well.

Vanilla - find one that has no glucose or other sugars/extra ingredients.

Eggs - use **large** pastured eggs.

Honey - I tend to use a cheap honey for baking as the nutrients are destroyed by heat. I measure this with a measuring cup. It will come out easier if you measure dry ingredients first.

Butter - Use grass-fed butter if possible, but if not, any butter is better than margarine. If you wish to substitute with coconut oil, please do. I find it easier to measure this with scales in ounces.

Measures:

My recipes are rather unusual as I use American cups for coconut flour/nuts and honey, whereas I use ounces for butter, as this is easier in the UK. If you do not have American cups, then 1 oz. of coconut flour is equal to 1/4 cup. 4 oz. of nuts is equal to 1 cup.

Chapter One

The icing on the cake

Serving suggestion: Chocolate celebration cake iced with chocolate butter icing (Page 8).

Icings

Icings are really easy once you get the idea. They are basically honey and butter mixed together: butter icing in the true sense of the word!

Start with soft butter and mix until it turns pale in colour. An electric hand mixer is ideal for this. Add in the other ingredients. If it is too soft, put it in the fridge for a short while to harden until it is workable. If it is stiff enough it can be piped.

Cakes iced with this icing will need to be kept in the fridge and served immediately once brought into room temperature, or the butter will melt if it gets too warm!!

Honey can be added according to how sweet you would like it, so diabetics are in total control. I only suggest quantities here for both butter and honey. You can make more/less as you require.

Vanilla Flavour:

3 oz. butter

2 tablespoons honey or to taste

1/2 teaspoon vanilla (make sure GAPS legal if necessary)

Lemon/Orange Flavour:

3 oz. butter

2 tablespoons honey or to taste

Rind of one organic, un-waxed, scrubbed lemon/orange plus 1 tablespoon lemon/orange juice.

Chocolate Flavour:

3 oz. butter

2 tablespoons honey or to taste

3 tablespoons cocoa powder

You could dust the cake with cocoa powder and/or shavings of 100% dark chocolate after icing.

Icings Continued

Fresh Fruit icing

Icings can also be made with fresh fruit, but would not keep so well.

Use 3 oz. butter and 3 tablespoons honey and mix in 1 tablespoon fresh/defrosted fruit:

strawberry, raspberry, blackberry, blueberry.

Toffee icing:

Melt 3 oz. butter in a pan with 1/4 cup honey. Bring to the boil and al-low   to bubble for 2 mins. Remove and let cool slightly before using to ice cakes.

Cream cheese frostings:

Soft cream cheese (if tolerated - not for GAPS diet) mixed with a little honey and vanilla makes a delicious topping, especially for the Carrot and Courgette cake.

If you are on the GAPS diet, you can make kefir cheese by dripping your milk kefir.

Chapter Two

Everyday cakes

Sizes and servings

Please note that all of these cakes, can be made as either:

- 12 individual small muffins

- **or** as one large 8 x 8 square cake

- **or** the mixture can be doubled and divided into two 7/8 inch round cake tins and iced in the middle.

or double the recipe and make a tray bake! Ideal for parties or larger gatherings.

The cooking time remains the same for all.

Storage

All of these cakes must be kept in an airtight container in the fridge. They will keep for up to week (if they last that long!)

Basic Muffin Recipe

This recipe forms the basis for all of the cakes. Most use diced courgette, others substitute soaked ground nuts instead of courgette. To this basic recipe can be added whatever you like. Once you have made some of my suggestions, why not experiment and see what you can make? The key is not to let the mixture become too dry. Ideally it should have a soft dropping consistency - like a batter. Add extra egg/s if need be. It is a very forgiving recipe. Always make sure the cake is fully cooked by inserting a knife into the centre. Once cooked, a knife should come out clean. If the cake sinks, then the mixture was too moist, if it cracks, then too dry.

Method:

Place courgette and coconut flour in food processor and blitz until finely chopped.

Add in melted butter, blitz again.

Add in eggs, honey and vanilla. Blitz to combine.

Lastly, add the bicarbonate of soda and briefly combine.

Divide between 12 cup cases.

Bake for 30 minutes Gas 6, 400 F., 200 c., 180 C. fan until a knife comes out clean.

Leave to cool and choose an icing if desired (see page 7). Store in an airtight container in the fridge for up to a week.

Ingredients:

1 cup diced courgette

1/2 cup coconut flour

3 oz. butter melted (3oz)

3 eggs

1/4 cup honey

1 teaspoon vanilla flavouring (ensure GAPS legal if necessary)

1/2 teaspoon bicarbonate of soda

Chocolate Cupcakes

Our family favourite and loved by many!

I've lost count of how many times I've been asked for the recipe!

Method:

Place courgette and coconut flour in food processor and blitz until finely chopped.

Add in coconut flour and cocoa powder, blitz briefly to combine.

Add in melted butter, blitz again.

Add in eggs, vanilla and honey. Blitz to combine.

Lastly, add the bicarbonate of soda and whizz briefly until combined.

Put a heaped desert spoonful of mixture into each cup case,

Bake for 30 minutes Gas 6, 400 F., 200 c., 180 C. fan until a knife comes out clean.

Leave to cool and choose an icing if desired (see page 7).

Store in an airtight container in the fridge.

Ingredients:

1 cup diced courgette

1/2 cup coconut flour

3oz butter melted

1/4 cup cocoa powder

1/4 cup honey

3 eggs

1 teaspoon vanilla flavouring (ensure GAPS legal if necessary)

1/2 teaspoon bicarbonate of soda

Lemon Muffins

Method:

Place courgette and coconut flour in food processor and blitz until finely chopped.

Add in butter, blitz again.

Add in eggs and honey. Blitz to combine.

Lastly, add the bicarb. of soda, lemon rind and juice and briefly combine.

Divide between 12 cup cases.

Bake for 30 minutes Gas 6, 400 F., 200 c., 180 C. fan until a knife comes out clean.

Leave to cool and choose an icing if desired (see page 7). A lemon icing goes well with these cakes. Store in an airtight container in the fridge.

Ingredients:

1 cup diced courgette

1/2 cup coconut flour

3 oz. butter melted (3oz)

3 eggs

1/4 cup honey

Rind of one scrubbed organic un-waxed lemon

2 tablespoons lemon juice

1/2 teaspoon bicarbonate of soda

Raisin Muffins

Here is another variation on the basic muffin mix. A plain butter icing goes well with these.

Method:

Place courgette and coconut flour in the food processor and blitz until finely chopped.

Add in melted butter, blitz again.

Add in eggs and honey. Blitz to combine.

Lastly, add the bicarb. of soda, vanilla and raisins and briefly combine.

Divide between 12 cup cases.

Bake for 30 minutes Gas 6, 400 F., 200 c., 180 C. fan until a knife comes out clean.

Leave to cool and choose an icing if desired (see page 7). Store in an airtight container in the fridge.

Ingredients:

1 cup diced courgette

1/2 cup coconut flour

3 oz. butter melted

3 eggs

1/4 cup honey

1 cup raisins

1 teaspoon vanilla (ensure GAPS legal)

1/2 teaspoon bicarbonate of soda

Sponge Pudding

Serving suggestion: This is like the Raisin Muffins, but served in a dish it makes a delicious, simple pudding.

Method:

Grease a 7 inch baking dish.

Melt butter in a small pan.

Meantime place courgette and coconut flour in the food processor and whiz until very fine. Scrape down sides as necessary..

Add in melted butter and blitz briefly to combine.

Add in eggs, vanilla, raisins and honey, blitz briefly.

Add in bicarbonate of soda and blitz briefly for the last time.

Pour into a 6/7 inch pie dish (or equivalent)

Bake for 30 minutes Gas 6, 400 F., 200 c., 180 C. fan until a knife comes out clean.

Slice and serve with sour cream or custard.

A delicious snack for a cool day!

Ingredients:

1 cup courgette , peeled, sliced and chopped into smaller pieces

1/2 cup coconut flour

3 eggs

1/2 cup butter melted (4oz)

1/4 cup honey, or less

1/2 cup raisins (more or less as you like)

1 teaspoon vanilla (ensure GAPS legal)

1/2 teaspoon bicarbonate of soda

Date and Lemon Slices

Method:

Grease and line an 8x8 baking tin.

Place courgettes and coconut flour in a food processor and whizz until fine and crumbly. Scrape down sides as necessary.

Place butter and dates in a saucepan together and heat until butter is bubbling. Allow it to bubble for 2 minutes, while mashing the dates in to the butter. Remove from heat and allow to cool slightly. Add to food processor and whizz together.

Ad eggs, lemon rind (grated), cacao nibs (if desired), sesame seeds, bicarb. of soda and whizz for last time.

Pour batter into prepared tin. Sprinkle with sesame seeds and cacao nibs if using.

Bake for 30 minutes Gas 6, 400 F., 200 c., 180 C. fan until a knife comes out clean.

Leave to cool. Store in an airtight container in the fridge.

Ingredients:

1 cup coconut flour

Rind of one lemon (un - waxed)

1 cup diced courgette

3 oz. butter melted

1/4 cup Sesame seeds plus more to sprinkle on top

1 cup dates

Cacao nibs (optional)

3 eggs

1/2 teaspoon bicarbonate of soda

Banana and Walnut Loaf

Perfect with a cup of coffee!

Method:

Grease a one pound loaf mould/tin.

Start by placing the dates in a bowl of boiling water for five minutes until soft and mushy. Then drain the water out.

Place courgette and coconut flour in food processor and blitz until finely chopped.

Add in melted butter, blitz again.

Add in eggs and drained dates. Blitz to combine.

Add the banana broken into small pieces.

Lastly, add the walnuts, bicarb. of soda and cinnamon and briefly combine.

Pour into a loaf mould.

Bake for 30 minutes Gas 6, 400 F., 200 c., 180 C. fan until a knife comes out clean.

Leave to cool and choose an icing if desired (see page 7). Store in an airtight container in the fridge.

Ingredients:

1 cup diced courgette

1/2 cup coconut flour

3 oz. cup butter melted

3 eggs

1 cup dates soaked

1 medium/large sized banana

1/4 cup walnuts

1/2 teaspoon bicarbonate of soda

1 teaspoon cinnamon

Apple Cake

Delicious with cream!

Method:

Place courgette and coconut flour in food processor and blitz until finely chopped.

Add in melted butter, blitz again.

Add in eggs and honey. Blitz to combine.

Lastly, add the bicarb. of soda and apple and briefly combine.

Pour into an 8x8 inch baking tin.

Bake for 30 minutes Gas 6, 400 F., 200 c., 180 C. fan until a knife comes out clean.

Leave to cool and serve with soured cream for the GAPS diet. Store in an airtight container in the fridge.

Ingredients:

1 cup diced courgette

1/2 cup coconut flour

3oz. butter melted

3 eggs

1/4 cup honey

1 large cooking apple finely chopped.

1/2 teaspoon bicarbonate of soda

Carrot and Courgette Cake

This is simply delicious! I could have eaten the whole cake in one sitting! Top with cream cheese frosting (page 8)!

Double the recipe to make a stunning two-tier celebration cake!

Method:

Place courgette, grated carrot and coconut flour in food processor and blitz until finely chopped. You may need to scrape down the sides a couple of times.

Add in the melted butter, blitz again.

Add in eggs and honey. Blitz to combine.

Add in the raisins and spices.

Lastly, add the bicarb. of soda and briefly combine.

Pour into an 8x8 inch baking tin. or individual muffin cases.

Bake for 30 minutes Gas 6, 400 F., 200 c., 180 C. fan or until a knife comes out clean.

Leave to cool and choose an icing if desired (see page 7). Store in an airtight container in the fridge.

Ingredients:

1 cup diced courgette

1 tightly packed cup grated carrot

1/2 cup coconut flour

3 oz. melted butter

3 eggs

1/4 cup honey

1/4 cup raisins

1/4 teaspoon mixed spice

1/4 teaspoon cinnamon

1/2 teaspoon bicarbonate of soda

Coffee and Walnut Cake

Method:

Make the coffee:

Grind some fresh coffee beans in a grinder. Put 3 heaped teaspoons of powder into a mug, and half fill with water. Allow to brew while you do the next bit.

Place courgette and coconut flour in the food processor and blitz until finely chopped. You may need to scrape down the sides a couple of times.

Add in the melted butter, blitz again.

Add in eggs and honey and 5 tablespoons of your coffee mixture. Blitz to combine.

Add in the walnuts and the bicarb. of soda and briefly combine.

Pour into an 8x8 inch baking tin. or individual muffin cases.

Bake for 30 minutes Gas 6, 400 F., 200 c., 180 C. fan or until a knife comes out clean.

Leave to cool and choose an icing if desired (see page 7). Store in an airtight container in the fridge.

Ingredients:

1 cup diced courgette

1/2 cup coconut flour + 1 tablespoon

3 oz. melted butter

3 heaped teaspoons fresh ground coffee beans, or if not on a healing diet, use coffee essence to taste

3 eggs

1/4 cup honey

1/4 cup walnuts

1/2 teaspoon bicarbonate of soda

Caramel Cake

This is lovely with a Toffee Icing - almost like fudge cake!

Method:

Place courgette and coconut flour in the food processor and blitz until finely chopped.

Place butter and dates in a pan and gently melt the butter while stirring the dates in, giving them a squash as they soften. Bring to the boil and boil for one minute.

Add the butter/date mixture to the food processor.

Add in eggs and cinnamon. Blitz to combine.

Lastly, add the bicarb. of soda and briefly combine.

Pour into an 8x8 inch baking tin, or individual muffin cases.

Bake for 30 minutes Gas 6, 400 F., 200 c., 180 C. fan until a knife comes out clean.

Leave to cool and ice with toffee butter icing (see page 7).

Store in an airtight container in the fridge for up to a week.

Ingredients:

1 cup diced courgette

1/2 cup coconut flour

3oz. melted butter

1 cup dates softened in boiling water

3 eggs

1 teaspoons cinnamon

1/2 teaspoon bicarbonate of soda

Orange and Coconut Cake

This goes well with orange icing!

Method:

Whizz the courgette and coconut flour together in the food processor until they resemble fine breadcrumbs.

Add in the melted butter, and whizz to combine.

Add in the eggs, orange juice and desiccated coconut and mix to combine - so that the coconut remains whole and doesn't get ground.

Add in the bicarb. of soda and mix briefly.

Pour the batter into an 8x8 square tin, or into individual muffin cases.

Bake for 30 minutes Gas 6, 400 F., 200 c., 180 C. fan or until a knife comes out clean.

Leave to cool and choose an icing if desired (see page 7).

Ingredients:

1 cup diced courgette

1/2 cup coconut flour

3oz. melted butter

3 eggs

1/4 cup desiccated coconut

Rind and juice of one large orange

1/2 teaspoon bicarbonate of soda

Coconut and Blueberry Muffins

This makes an interestingly coloured cake - blue! Maybe not one for my nephew who eyes all my grain-free cakes with suspicion as to their ingredients! Try different berries to find your favourite.

Method:

Place courgette and coconut flour in food processor and blitz until finely chopped.

Add in butter, blitz again.

Add in eggs and honey. Blitz to combine.

Add in the coconut and the blueberries and mix.

Lastly, add the bicarb. of soda and briefly combine.

Pour into an 8x8 inch baking tin, or individual muffin cases.

Bake for 30 minutes Gas 6, 400 F., 200 c., 180 C. fan until a knife comes out clean.

Ingredients:

1 cup diced courgette

1/2 cup coconut flour

3 oz. butter melted

3 eggs

1/4 cup honey

1/2 cup desiccated coconut (preservative free for GAPS)

1/4 cup frozen blueberries (or other frozen berry - experiment!)

1/2 teaspoon bicarbonate of soda

Mince Pie Muffins

If you want cake with a seasonal flavour, then look no further! I can imagine them served warm in custard........ Mmmmmmm! Best warm from the oven.

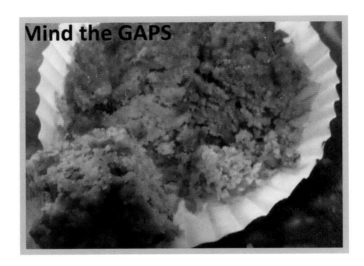

Method:

Whizz the courgette and coconut flour together in the food processor until they resemble fine breadcrumbs.

Add the butter, whizz again.

Add the eggs and whizz until mixed in.

Add the fruit and spices and baking soda

Mix one last time.

Spoon into 12 muffin cases .

Bake for 30 minutes Gas 6, 400 F., 200 c., 180 C. fan or until a knife comes out clean.

Leave to cool and choose an icing if desired (see page 7).

Store in the fridge in an airtight container for up to a week.

Ingredients:

1 cup diced courgette
1/2 cup coconut flour
2oz. butter (solid)
3 eggs
rind of one un-waxed lemon
1 tablespoon fresh pressed orange juice
1 desert apple finely chopped
4 oz. currants/raisins (the amount is not over-ly important, a cupful will do)
1/2 teaspoon cinnamon
1/2 teaspoon mixed spice
1/2 teaspoon bicarbonate of soda

Chapter Four

Celebration Cakes

Perfect for a birthday or other celebration.

For all chocolate lovers!

Celebration Cake!

Method:

Place courgette and coconut flour in food processor and blitz until finely chopped.

Add in coconut flour and cocoa powder, blitz briefly to combine.

Add in melted butter, blitz again.

Add in eggs and honey. Blitz to combine.

Lastly, add the baking soda and whizz briefly until combined.

Divide equally between two 8 inch cake tins. Bake for 30 minutes Gas 6, 400 F., 200 c., 180 C. fan until a knife comes out clean.

Leave to cool.

Coat generously inside and on top with a double recipe of chocolate butter icing. Sometimes we add sliced fruit and nut bars, but you can sprinkle with cocoa powder and add cacao nibs, or decorate with plain and chocolate icing.

Once iced, store in a refrigerator for up to a week.

Ingredients:

2 cups diced courgette

1 cup coconut flour

6oz. butter melted

1/2 cup cocoa powder

1/2 cup honey

6 eggs

1 teaspoon baking soda

If your food processor is very small, you can transfer the mixture to a bowl once you have blitzed the courgette and coconut flour, and use a wooden spoon to mix in the other ingredients.

Fruit Cake

There is no courgette in this cake. No-one will ever know that this cake is not made from flour - unless you tell them. Moist and rich, it could be served for any special occasion, or just to spoil yourself. Be warned. One slice won't be enough!

Due to the amount of dried fruit used in this recipe, it may not be suitable for diabetics.

This cake requires the nuts and dried fruit to be soaked for 2 hours before making the cake.

Fruit Cake cont..

Method:

Start 2 hours before hand. Soak the cashews in a bowl of water for 2 hours, then place the dried fruit in a saucepan and cover with boiling water. Place a lid on the pan and let sit until you are ready to make the cake.

Place the nuts in the food processor and whizz until they resemble fine bread crumbs.

Add the coconut flour and whizz again to incorporate.

Ad the melted butter, briefly whizz again.

Add the eggs and briefly mix again.

Add the spices, and mix briefly.

Add the dried fruit and orange rind, mix to combine - briefly.

Finally add the bicarbonate of soda and mix to combine.

Pour into an 8in. lined, round tin.

Bake for 30 minutes Gas 6, 400 F., 200 c., 180 C. fan. After 30 minutes, check the cake.. If the top is browning too much, put a layer of baking paper over it to prevent burning and bake until a knife inserted into the middle of the cake comes out clean.

Ingredients:

(In the order to be used in the *Method*)

1 cup cashews soaked for at least 2 hours

1 cup sultanas

1 cup currants

1/2 cup coconut flour

3 oz. butter melted

3 large pastured eggs

Grated rind of one large orange (can be omitted if desired)

1 teaspoon mixed spice

1 teaspoon cinnamon

1 teaspoon bicarbonate of soda